MYSTERIES

OF THE ANCIENT WORLD

THE EASTER ISLAND ENIGMA

PAUL G. BAHN

WEIDENFELD & NICOLSON
LONDON

The small speck of land now known as Easter Island is one of the most remote pieces of permanently inhabited land in the world. Roughly triangular in shape, it is entirely volcanic in origin, and covers only 171 square km in the South Pacific. Yet this seemingly insignificant place has caused a huge amount of ink to flow, thanks to the amazing Stone Age culture that once filled it with enormous stone statues, many of them set up on massive stone platforms. It has often been presented to the world at large, in popular books and television documentaries, as a place full of mysteries – but research by archaeologists and others over the course of this century has finally solved most of the island's enigmas.

*E**aster Island as seen from space.
The craters of Rano Kau and
Rano Raraku are clearly visible.*

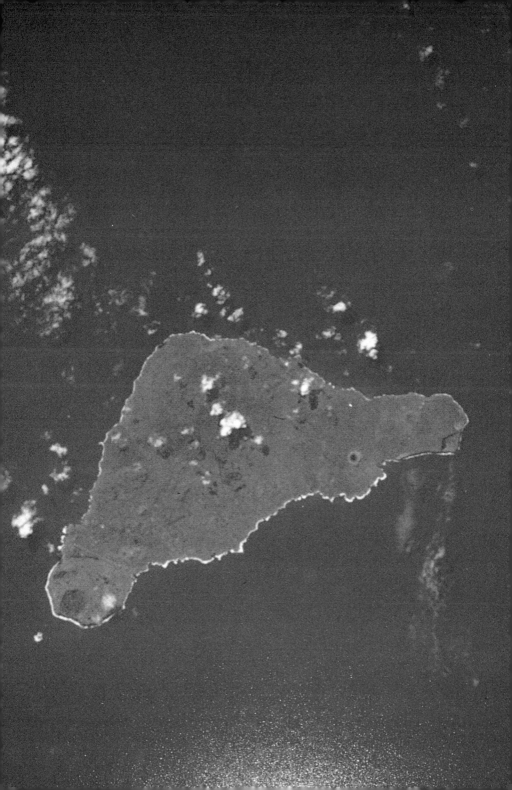

The First Inhabitants

The island is now generally known as Rapa Nui (Big Rapa) since 19th-century Tahitian sailors felt it resembled a large version of the Polynesian island of Rapa. It is so remote – 3,747 km from South America and 3,622 km from Pitcairn Island to the northwest – that it is extremely unlikely that it was ever colonized more than once by people arriving in canoes, and certainly the archaeological record indicates a single unbroken development of culture from the first settlers until the arrival of Europeans. Radiocarbon dating together with evidence from linguistics, suggests that people first came here in the early centuries AD (although some researchers now believe that the arrival was some centuries later), and by the 7th century their stone structures were already well developed. Contrary to theories put forward by several people over the years, and most obsessively and persistently by Norwegian adventurer Thor Heyerdahl, the island's colonists did *not* come from South America, but rather from eastern Polynesia, almost certainly the Marquesas Islands. This is confirmed not only by archaeology and language, but also anthropology, blood groups and genetics.

*F*inished statues, inside the crater of Rano Raraku, stand facing the crater lake.

Once they had reached the remote island, they were trapped there, and it constituted their whole world. Their first known contact with the rest of humanity came on Easter Sunday (5 April) 1722, when the Dutch navigator Jacob Roggeveen encountered the island, and gave it its current name. He and two of his companions were also the first to leave us written descriptions of the inhabitants. Subsequent 18th-century visitors included such famous explorers as Captain Cook and the Comte de La

*T**he islanders constructed garden enclosures called 'manavai' (place of water) to protect crops from the ferocious winds.***

Pérouse. All of these early accounts of Easter Island marvel at the huge statues and wonder how such an apparently primitive people could move and erect such wonders on an island with no timber.

Archaeological investigation of the island began in the late 19th century, but really came into its own in 1955 when a Norwegian expedition, led by Heyerdahl, came here, bringing in professional archaeologists. This expedition was important not only for carrying out the first stratigraphic excavations and obtaining the first radiocarbon dates and pollen samples, but also for conducting valuable experiments in carving, moving and erecting statues with the help of the islanders.

*H*oles left in lava by the
now-vanished trunks of
large trees, the island's extinct
giant palm, one species in the
now vanished rainforest.

However, it was new analyses of pollen obtained in cores from the sediments at the bottom of the freshwater lakes in the island's great volcanic craters (Rano Kau, Rano Raraku, Rano Aroi) which led British palaeobotanist John Flenley in the 1980s to discover that the island was originally covered by a rainforest dominated by a species of huge palm tree very similar to *Jubaea chilensis*, the Chilean wine palm, the largest in the world.

It was to this island, totally different in appearance from that of today, that there came a group of Polynesian voyagers – probably a few dozen men, women and children in one or more big double-hulled canoes – bringing with them the domestic animals (chickens, rats, pigs and dogs) and food plants (bananas, sweet potatoes, taro, breadfruit) with which they transformed the environment of so many Polynesian islands. Breadfruit, however, could not grow in Easter Island's climate, while pigs and dogs – if they ever arrived – did not survive long; their bones have never been found.

The colonists set about changing the landscape – making clearings in the forest to plant their crops. The island's native birds, unused to humans, were an easy prey to hunters, while the newly arrived rats stole their eggs and their young, so the few remaining seabirds retreated to the small islets offshore.

During this initial phase, the islanders seem to have constructed small, simple *ahu* (stone platforms) of normal Polynesian type, with small and relatively crude statues upon or in front of them.

The Construction of the Statues

In the second or 'middle' phase of Easter Island's history, seen as its Golden Age, from *circa* AD 1000 to 1500, an enormous amount of human energy and effort was poured into the construction of more and bigger ceremonial platforms (comprising cores of rubble encased with often well-cut stone slabs) and

*T*he well-fitted stonework of the Vinapu I platform on the island's south coast has often been compared erroneously with the utterly different Inka stonework of Peru.

hundreds of large statues. As the human population thrived – apparently living in peace, since there are no weapons in the archaeological record – numbers must have increased, perhaps quite rapidly: some speculate that a peak of 10,000 or even 20,000 was reached by *c.* AD 1500. This led to greater pressure on the supply of land, and the need for ever increasing quantities of food. The inevitable decline of the forest, as more land was cleared, can be seen in the record of fossilized pollen from the crater swamps. At the same time, the increasing pace and quantity of statue carving required ever greater amounts of timber for rollers and levers.

At least 800 *moai* (statues) were carved, nearly all of them in the soft, volcanic tuff of the Rano Raraku crater, with basalt hammerstones – thousands of which were left lying in the quarry. All of the statues were variations on a theme, a human figure with a prominent, angular nose and chin, and often elongated perforated ears containing disks. The bodies, which end at the abdomen, have arms held tightly to the sides, and hands held in front, with

A **erial view of the crater of Rano Kau.**

long fingertips meeting a stylized loincloth. They are believed to represent ancestor figures.

More than 230 *moai* were transported considerable distances from the great quarry to platforms around the edge of the island, where they were erected, with their backs to the sea, watching over the villages around each platform. It is possible that some were floated on rafts

*V**iew to the coast from the outer slope of the Rano Raraku quarry, showing a few of the numerous finished statues scattered around it.*

*S**tatue on the outer slope of Rano Raraku with a European three-masted sailing ship engraved on its chest.*

*T*he long tapering fingers on this statue at Anakena make its hands look almost like wings.

13

*T*he great coastal ahu *of Tongariki, reconstructed in the 1990s. The statue in the foreground had its base damaged in an experiment to see if the statues could have been swivelled to their final destination in an upright position.*

14

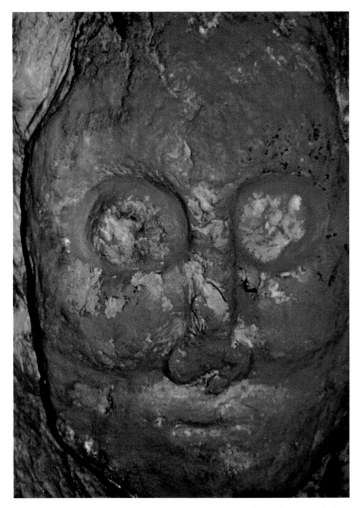

A large bas-relief
of Makemake,
the creator god,
painted bright red,
inside one of the
caves on Motu Nui.

T he backs
of the statues
at Ahu Nau Nau,
Anakena, display
intricate carved
spiral patterns in
bas-relief.

around the coast to their platform. For the rest, it has traditionally been suggested that they were dragged horizontally to their destinations, their path lubricated with mashed palm fronds and sweet potatoes. However, recent experiments have shown that another efficient mode of transportation was upright on a sledge and rollers.

At the most prestigious platforms, the statues were given a separate *pukao* or topknot of red scoria, raised and placed on the head; and eyes of white coral,

which seem to have been inserted at certain times or ceremonies to 'activate' the statues' *mana* or spiritual power. The existence of these eyes was only discovered in the 1980s; and when replicas are fitted into the sockets on re-erected statues, it transforms their appearance. The statues did not stare at the villages, but rather, their gaze was slightly upward, which may explain an old name for the island, Mata-ki-te-Rangi (eyes towards the heavens).

The statues placed on platforms range from 2 to 10 m in height, and weigh up to 83,000 kg. The biggest platform was Tongariki, whose fallen remains were smashed and scattered in 1960 by a tidal wave (*tsunami*), triggered by an earthquake in Chile – indeed, its 15 great statues, up to 30 tonnes apiece, were

The Ahu Nau Nau, at Anakena, showing the statues with their stone topknots restored to them, and with reproduction eyes in place.

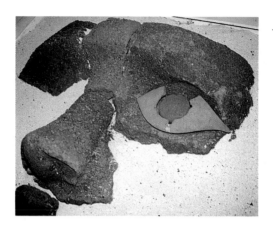

An original eye placed in the socket of a statue fragment in the island's museum.

The monstrous 'El Gigante', the biggest moai *ever carved, still lies unfinished in the quarry.*

*S*unset at
*Ahu Ko Te
Riku, Tahai.*

carried about 90 m inland from the platform by the wave. This platform was restored in the 1990s.

The quarry at Rano Raraku still contains almost 400 statues on and around its inner and outer slopes, in every stage of manufacture. One of them, 'El Gigante', is over 20 m long, and when completed would have weighed up to 274,000 kg. Many doubt that even the ingenious islanders could have moved this colossus, had it been completed, let alone have erected it.

It is the finished statues that stand on the quarry's slopes (many more probably lie buried and undiscovered here), and they have been covered by

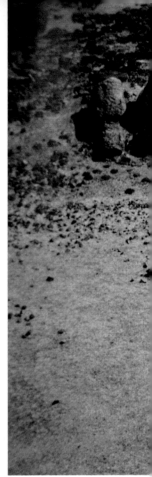

*A*erial shot of the fallen statues of the Ahu Vaihu.

*S*ome of the thousands of obsidian mataa – dagger or spearheads – which reflect the rise of violence on the island.

accumulated sediments up to their necks over time, and hence have given rise to the popular misconception of 'Easter Island heads', so beloved of cartoonists. They are all, in fact, full statues down to the abdomen.

The Decline of a Civilization

The final phase of the island's prehistory saw the collapse of the earlier way of life: statues ceased to be carved, cremation gave way to burial, and 1,000 years of peaceful coexistence were shattered by the manufacture in huge quantities of *mataa*, spearheads and daggers of obsidian, a sharp, black volcanic glass. Conflict seems to have led to the toppling of the statues – some researchers

have recently suggested that an earthquake might have been at least partially responsible, but there is no evidence of this at all in the island's folk-tales, and such a shattering experience in such recent times would certainly have left its mark in legend and song, as the human strife did.

The conflict was resolved by an apparent abandonment of the earlier religion and social system based on ancestor worship, in favour of one featuring a warrior elite. An annual chief or 'birdman' was chosen each year at the ceremonial village of Orongo, whose drystone corbelled houses were perched high on the cliff separating the great Rano Kau crater from the ocean. Each candidate had a young man to represent him. Every spring, these unfortunate young

*R**ock carvings of the birdman on the cliffs at Orongo, with a view of the islets Motu Nui and Motu Iti.*

*T**he great crater of Rano Kau, a caldera formed by the collapse of a volcanic cone. The swamp is a thin, floating mat of vegetation, into which at least one geologist has already disappeared without trace.*

men had to descend the sheer cliff 300 m high, to the shore, then swim over a kilometre on a bunch of reeds through shark-infested swells and strong currents to the largest and outermost islet, Motu Nui, where they awaited – sometimes for weeks – the arrival of a migratory seabird, the sooty tern. The aim was to find its first egg. The winner would swim back with the egg securely held in a headband, and his master would become the new sacred birdman. Orongo's rich rock art is festooned with carvings of the birdmen, sometimes holding the egg, which symbolized fertility. This was the system that was still developing when the Europeans turned up, and which ended with the arrival of missionaries in the 1860s.

Cross-section of one of the houses at Orongo showing the thickness of the drystone walls, the corbelled vault and the capping of stone slabs and earth. Motu Nui is visible offshore.

Part of the profusion of rock art at Orongo, with birdmen carved everywhere in various orientations.

A carving of a birdman, with vulva motifs, from Orongo: 46 cm high, 31 cm wide, 23 cm thick.

27

Rongorongo

It seems to have been the arrival of Europeans which brought about Easter Island's last great mystery, the famous *rongorongo* writing, since we have no evidence of its existence before that time. The script comprises parallel lines of characters, many of them bird symbols, hooks, etc., engraved on wooden

The **rongorongo** **tablet known as** *the 'Echancrée'.*   tablets. Every alternate line is upside down, and the overall impression is of a tightly packed mass of uniform, skilfully inscribed hieroglyphics. Not one of the early European visitors who came to the island after its discovery by the outside world in 1722 ever mentioned the wooden tablets or the characters,

*V*iew out of the cave of Ana Kai Tangata (which means 'eat men cave' or perhaps 'cave that eats men' or 'cave where men eat'!), showing the wall paintings of terns.

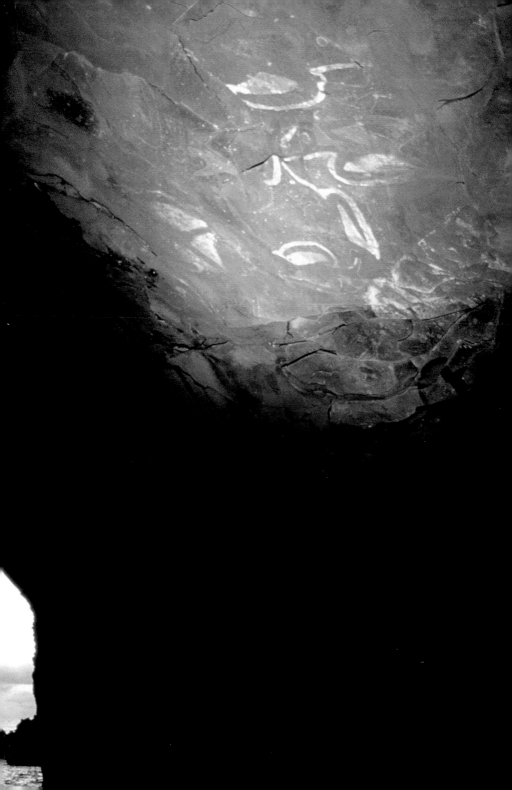

although some spent days exploring ashore and entered native houses. The earliest written mention of the phenomenon is by a missionary in 1864, who said they were to be found in every house. Later visitors reported that they were kept apart in special houses and were very strictly taboo. It seems most likely that the 'script' was a very late phenomenon, directly inspired by the visit of the Spanish in 1770, when a written proclamation of annexation was offered to the chiefs and priests to be 'signed in their native characters'. This was probably their first experience of speech embodied in parallel lines, and they then adopted a method of 'script' that used motifs they had already been using in their rich rock art – the birds, fishes, turtles, vulvas, and other motifs in the rock art inventory also form part of the inscriptions. The signs were first lightly etched on the wood with sharp flakes of obsidian (volcanic glass) to provide an outline, and then deeply incised with a dull shark's tooth.

The script now survives only as markings on 25 pieces of wood – in pre-missionary days they were often destroyed in wars or deliberately burned, others were buried with the honoured dead, and it is possible that many were hidden in sacred caves to protect these symbols of paganism after the arrival of Christianity on the island. The known specimens, all housed in museums, contain a total of over 14,000 glyphs (or hieroglyphs) – ranging from one artefact with only two glyphs incised on it, to 2,300 on another. The island's *rongorongo* experts escaped the slave raids of 1862/3 which took numerous islanders off to Peru, but they died in the subsequent smallpox epidemic, and this is why the tablets' content has largely remained a mystery.

A major breakthrough in cracking the *rongorongo* code was recently achieved by Steven Fischer, a specialist in linguistics and epigraphy. The 'Rosetta Stone' in his decipherment was the Santiago Staff, a 2 kg wooden sceptre acquired by

THE EASTER ISLAND ENIGMA

*T*he Santiago Staff (above) whose
rongorongo glyphs proved a Rosetta Stone
for Steven Fischer's decipherment. Note the
vertical lines scattered through the text.

*S*ome rongorongo-script
characters (below)
from the Santiago Staff.

Chileans in 1870; measuring 126 cm by 6.5 cm, it once belonged to an Easter Island *ariki* or leader. Fischer discovered that this staff, uniquely among *rongorongo* inscriptions, marks textual divisions with about 97 irregularly spaced vertical lines; and he also noticed that each glyph that starts a new division (i.e. is immediately to the right of a vertical line) is suffixed with a phallus-like motif; and in the series of glyphs within each division, almost every third one (the 4th, 7th, 10th, 13th, etc.) also has this phallic suffix. Not one division has the suffix on its last or its penultimate glyph; not one division contains fewer than 3 glyphs; most divisions comprise multiples of three, and the first in each trio sports a huge phallus in almost every case. In other words, the Santiago Staff has a basic triad structure, which also seems to occur on some other *rongorongo* artefacts. Based on a recitation by an old islander in 1886, and on our knowledge of ancient Polynesian beliefs, Fischer has concluded that the *rongorongo* inscriptions on which he has detected the triad structure are cosmogonies (creation chants) – a whole succession of copulations (each triad denoting that X copulated with Y and the result was Z) to explain the creation of everything in the world. Among the other inscriptions, one appears to be a calendar text of some sort, as was discovered in the 1950s, and then there are anomalous groupings of signs that still have to be identified as to genre. The *rongorongo* script still retains much of its mystery.

What Happened to Easter Island

It is impossible now to know exactly what happened on Easter Island. However, the probably steady growth of the population together with the decline in food and increased importance of economically useless activities (platform building, statue carving and transportation) seem to have led to a collapse.

The famous kneeling statue 'Tukuturi' was discovered in 1955 on the outer flank of the Rano Raraku quarry. Some see this as an early prototype of the moai, others as a very late sculpture.

A **four-masted
schooner at
anchor off the coast
beyond a moai on
the platform of
Ahu Ko Te Riku
at Tahai.**

The causes of the island's decline and change were probably complex – it is possible that the climatic episode known as the 'Little Ice Age' may have played a role – but even the far greater climatic changes of the earlier Ice Age proper did not have an impact anything like the arrival of humans. The major factor in the island's collapse was clearly the human colonization. Pollen analysis has revealed here the most dramatic deforestation known in the archaeological record. From at least 1,200 years ago one can see a massive reduction in forest cover until, by the time Europeans arrived, there were no large trees left. The imported rats fed on the palm fruits and helped prevent regenerations. Without the palm and other timber, statues could no longer be moved (hence the abandonment of work in the quarry); ocean-going canoes could no longer be built, thus cutting the population off from the crucial protein supply of deep-sea fish; and deforestation also caused massive soil erosion which damaged crop-growing potential. Chickens became the most precious source of protein, guarded like treasure in fortified structures. Starvation gave rise to raiding and violence, and perhaps even to cannibalism.

By 1722, when Europeans arrived, it was virtually over. The population had been reduced to about 2,000, living in poverty amid the ruins of their former culture. The palm tree and several other species became extinct, leaving the island with only one small species of tree and two of shrubs. Subsequent slave-raids and epi-

Engraving made on the 1786 French expedition to the island. The Comte de la Pérouse is shown measuring a statue with its pukao still in place.

demics eventually reduced the population to just over 100, wiping out almost all of the ruling and priestly clans who could have revealed so much of the island's culture, and of its *rongorongo*. Instead we have had to build up a picture from the stunted testimony of the descendants of these few survivors, from archaeological and palaeo-environmental investigations and from experimentation. Our knowledge of what happened on Easter Island is far from perfect, and will certainly change as more evidence comes to light. But at least we have a clear idea of the unimaginable cultural achievements and ingenuity, as well as the environmental shortsightedness of that unique island's remarkable population.

PHOTOGRAPHIC ACKNOWLEDGEMENTS

Cover Paul Bahn [PB]; page 3 Nasa; pp. 4–5 PB;
p. 6tl Georgia Lee [GL]; p. 6tr John Flenley;
pp. 8–9 PB; pp. 10–11 William D. Hyde [WDH];
p. 12t PB; p. 12b WDH; p. 13 PB;
pp. 14–15 Catherine Orliac; p. 16 GL;
p. 17 WDH; p. 18 GL; p. 19t PB; p. 19b GL;
pp. 20–21 PB; pp. 22bl, 22–3t André Cuénot
[AC]; pp. 245. 25, 26 PB; p. 27t GL; p. 27b PB;
pp. 28–9 AC; pp. 30–31 Mark Oliver; p. 33t AC;
pp. 34, 36–7 GL; p. 39 E.T. Archive.

THE
EASTER
ISLAND
ENIGMA

First published in Great Britain 1997
by George Weidenfeld and Nicolson Ltd
The Orion Publishing Group
5 Upper St Martin's Lane
London WC2H 9EA

Text copyright © Paul G. Bahn, 1997
The moral right of the author has been asserted
Design and layout copyright © George Weidenfeld
and Nicolson Ltd, 1997

A CIP catalogue record for this book is available
from the British Library
ISBN 0 297 823035

Picture Research: Joanne King

Design: Harry Green

Typeset in Baskerville